BOOK ANALYSIS

By Jim Hilton

The Maltese Falcon

by Dashiell Hammett

DASHIELL HAMMETT

AMERICAN WRITER

- **Born in St Mary's County, Maryland (United States) in 1894.**
- **Died in Manhattan, New York City in 1961.**
- **Notable works:**
  - *Red Harvest* (1929), novel
  - *The Glass Key* (1931), novel
  - *The Thin Man* (1934), novel

Dashiell Hammett was an American writer of crime stories and novels, and a pioneer of the 'hard-boiled' genre. Mostly set in America's inner-city underworld, his stories were often morbidly violent, while his heroes were cynical and world-weary figures. The protagonist of Hammett's third novel, P.I. Sam Spade in *The Maltese Falcon* (1930), was played by Humphrey Bogart (American actor, 1899-1957) in the 1941 film adaptation, and the role helped to establish Bogart as Hollywood's quintessential noir detective. Bogart would go on to play the famous P.I. Philip Marlowe in the 1946 film adaptation of Raymond Chandler's (American writer, 1888-1959) *The Big Sleep* (1939). Unlike many of his contemporaries, Hammett had first-hand experience of the gritty underworld his stories described. For seven years, Hammett worked as an operative for the Pinkerton National Detective Agency. Across the late 19th and early 20th centuries, the Pinkertons were employed as strike-breakers: they would spy on and infiltrate unions and attempt to bring them down from the inside. Hammett was left deeply jaded by this employment and over the rest of his life he moved further and further to the political left. Like so many of his peers, he became a victim of McCarthyism in the 1950s, when he was investigated by the House Un-American Activities Committee and was subsequently blacklisted.

THE MALTESE FALCON

HAMMETT'S STYLISH CRIME CAPER STILL PACKS A PUNCH

- **Genre:** novel
- **Reference edition:** Hammett, D. (2010) *The Maltese Falcon.* London: Orion.
- **1st edition:** 1930 (serialised from 1929)
- **Themes:** betrayal, wealth, violence, masculinity, the American Dream

The Maltese Falcon was originally serialised in the crime magazine *Black Mask* between 1929 and 1930, before being published in book form in 1930 by Alfred A. Knopf. The first film adaptation came out as early as 1931, while another followed in 1936 (this one titled *Satan Met a Lady*). But the best-loved version of Hammett's novel is surely the 1941 film directed by John Huston (American film director, 1906-1987). Huston's first film, *The Maltese Falcon* (1941) starred Humphrey Bogart in what would be a career-defining role as P.I. Sam Spade, and was an early example of the 1940s American film genre that would come to be known as 'film noir'.

As a crime novel, *The Maltese Falcon* is something between a labyrinth and a merry-go-round. Its various wheeling components can be difficult to keep track of, and every character seems to depend on deception to some varying degree. Our only constant, our rock, as we move through San Francisco's proliferation of hotels, is Hammett's hero: Private Investigator Sam Spade. When a young woman calling herself Miss Wonderly pays Spade and his partner Miles Archer 200 dollars to follow a man named Thursby, on a rather flimsy pretext, Spade and Archer are curious. By the second chapter, Archer has been shot dead on the job and it is up to Spade to solve his partner's murder and put himself in the clear, as San Francisco's police department grows increasingly weary of his attitude. What begins as a straightforward detective story soon turns into just one cold-blooded chapter of a great historical treasure-hunt: the search for the Maltese Falcon.

SUMMARY

CHAPTERS 1-2

P.I. Sam Spade receives a visit from a woman called Miss Wonderly. She tells Spade that her younger sister has run off with a man called Floyd Thursby, and she is worried that this Thursby is dangerous. Miss Wonderly even flinches when the door opens – but it is only Miles Archer, Spade's partner. She has organized to meet Thursby that night at around 8 o'clock, and wants to have him followed. She gives the detectives two hundred-dollar bills, and they agree to take the job on.

Later that night, Spade is woken by a telephone call from his police buddy, Tom Polhaus, informing him that Archer has been found dead – gunned down. Spade joins Polhaus at the crime scene. He tells Polhaus about Floyd Thursby, but leaves out the specifics and does not mention Miss Wonderly.

Spade ducks into a drug-store and calls up Effie Perine, his secretary, telling her the news and asking her to inform Archer's wife Iva, before heading back home. He mixes himself a drink, but his door-bell rings shortly afterwards: it is Tom Polhaus and Lieutenant Dundy. Dundy demands to know the identity of Spade's client, and finally reveals that "just thirty-five minutes" after Spade left the crime-scene, Floyd Thursby was shot dead outside his hotel (p. 18). Dundy suspects Spade of killing Thursby, but promises he will investigate it fairly.

CHAPTERS 3-6

The next morning, Spade finds Archer's widow Iva waiting for him in his office. We infer that the two have been lovers: Iva kisses him and asks Spade earnestly whether he killed Archer. He refuses to engage and Iva heads home. Effie, a little jealous, suspects that Iva killed Archer herself so as to marry Spade, but Spade is sceptical of the idea.

Spade finds that Miss Wonderly has already checked out of her hotel, but when he returns to his office, he finds a message from her: she is staying at another hotel, the Coronet, under the name of Miss LeBlanc.

Spade heads to the Coronet, and Miss Wonderly confesses that she made up the story about her sister. Her real name is Brigid O'Shaughnessy. Brigid begs Spade to protect her from the police and from some other danger, but she is still not willing to confide in him. She claims that she and Thursby met in Hong Kong, and that she put her trust in him, but that he betrayed her. She firmly denies having anything to do with the murders, and Spade finally agrees to do his best to help her, for a further 500 dollars.

Later that day, a man called Joel Cairo shows up at Spade's. Cairo tells Spade that he would like to pay him 5000 dollars for the recovery of a "statuette" – "the black figure of a bird" (p. 41). At this point, Effie pokes her head through the door to announce that she's going home. When Spade turns back to his guest, he sees that Cairo is pointing "a short compact flat black pistol" squarely in his direction (p. 42).

Cairo means to search Spade's office for the bird, but as he attempts to frisk Spade, our hero manages to elbow him and snatch the gun, before punching him and knocking him out. Spade goes through Cairo's pockets, before the man eventually comes to. Much to Spade's surprise, Cairo repeats his offer of 5000 dollars for the safe delivery of the bird, but will give Spade no clues as to the identity of his employer. Spade accepts 200 dollars as "a retainer", and then returns Cairo his gun (p. 47). With his weapon back, Cairo repeats his intention to search Spade's office, and Spade, amused at Cairo's dedication, does not try to stop him.

After Cairo's visit, Spade walks into town, and notices a "youth of twenty or twenty-one" who seems to be tailing him (p. 50). Spade catches Cairo again on his way into a theatre on Geary Street, and indicating the lurking youth, asks Cairo who he is. Cairo claims not to know him. Spade boards a tram-car and finally manages to lose the youth, before paying a visit to Brigid at the Coronet.

Spade tells Brigid that he has met Joel Cairo, and Brigid seems unnerved by the fact. He tells her about the 5000 dollar offer, and tries to make her give him more information, but she once again puts him off – simply asking him to trust her. He suggests a meeting with the three of them at his apartment later that night, and she agrees. They take a taxi back to Spade's apartment, where he finds Iva sitting outside in her car – jealous and strung out. Spade tells her to go home.

CHAPTERS 7-9

Once he and Brigid are inside, Spade calls Cairo's hotel and leaves a message instructing him to come over. Sitting down together, Spade – out of nowhere – begins to tell Brigid the story of a case he worked on some years ago as a detective in Seattle. A man named Flitcraft had disappeared one day without a trace, leaving a wife and children. Five years later, a man fitting Flitcraft's description was spotted in Spokane, and Spade went to speak with him. The man, now going by the name Charles Pierce, was indeed the same man. Now he owned an automobile-business, and had a new family. The story he gave Spade was that one day, he had been walking down the street when a beam suddenly fell from a construction site above him, grazing his cheek. In that moment, all the arbitrariness and contingency of life was violently brought home to him; however careful a citizen or good a husband he was, he could die at any minute. It occurred to him that life should embrace that chaotic tendency and not attempt to stifle it. So he decided to change lives, randomly and with no warning. But what really fascinates Spade is that as soon as Flitcraft changed lives, he fell back into exactly the same pattern: the business, wife, children and the suburban house. He did not seem to realise that he was doing it all the same again.

Cairo finally arrives from the theatre and reports that the young man is staking out the apartment from the street. Brigid tells Cairo that she does not have the bird, but that she believes she knows where it is, or rather where Thursby left it. Cairo asks her what happened to Thursby and Brigid, suggestively, draws a figure "G" in the air. The two are just beginning to fight when there is suddenly a ring at the bell.

Spade goes to answer the door, telling the others to be quiet. It is Tom Polhaus and Lieutenant Dundy. Spade refuses to let them through the door, while Dundy hits him with the allegation that Spade and Iva have been having an affair, with the implication that Spade arranged Archer's death. Spade manages to put them off, before a cry of "Help! Help! Police! Help!" (p. 70) from Joel Cairo and the sound of scuffling next door makes them barge through.

Cairo and Brigid both claim the other assaulted them, and Dundy is preparing to take everyone into custody when Spade makes the manifestly bogus claim that the whole thing was just a joke they were playing. Wanting to avoid arrest, Brigid and Cairo enthusiastically back Spade up, and agree that they were only fighting in jest. Tom and Dundy leave angrily and Cairo goes out with them.

Spade asks Brigid what happened with her and Cairo, but she is evasive. He renews his questioning about the bird and about Thursby, and Brigid tells him a vague tale about being offered 500 pounds to steal the statue from a Russian in Constantinople, but Spade senses she is lying again. It is now late into the night and the two of them kiss.

CHAPTERS 10-12

The next morning, while Brigid is still asleep, Spade borrows her hotel-room key and searches her room at the Coronet, but finds no sign of the bird. He comes back to the apartment, picking up breakfast on the way, and the two eat together, before Spade drops Brigid back at her hotel.

Next he goes to Joel Cairo's hotel, but finds Cairo out. Instead he finds the loitering youth reading a paper in the lobby and confronts him, asking where "G" is, but the youth is uncooperative. Cairo finally arrives and informs Spade that he has spent the whole night being questioned by the police, but maintains that he has not told them anything. Spade returns to his office, where he learns that "G" has called for him, and finds Brigid, who is distressed after finding that her hotel room has been searched. Spade feigns ignorance in the matter, and organises for Brigid to be put up at Effie's house for a few days.

The telephone rings and it is none other than "G" himself: Mr Casper Gutman. The two organise to meet at Gutman's hotel, the Alexandria, in 15 minutes. Just as Spade is preparing to leave, Iva comes in, apologising. It was she who called Polhaus and Dundy over to Spade's apartment last night out of jealousy. Frustrated, and sensing further problems from the police, Spade tells Iva to get her story straight and go and talk to his lawyer, Sid Wise.

Spade arrives at the Alexandria and is received amicably. Gutman enquires whom Spade is working for and Spade is non-committal. Gutman gives the impression that the bird is worth far more than the money than the others have been willing to admit, but will not be drawn on details. Spade pretends that he knows where the bird is, and attempts to leverage Gutman into telling him *what* the bird is – finally giving Gutman an ultimatum of 5:30 that day.

Spade heads to his lawyer, Sid Wise's office. Wise relays what Iva told him: that she was not at home on the night that her husband was killed; that she started off spying on him (Archer), and then started looking for Spade. Spade does not know whether to believe it or not, but decides that it is functional as an alibi.

Spade gets back to his office, where Effie is waiting. She informs him that Brigid never arrived at her place. Spade gets hold of the taxi driver who was meant to drive Brigid there, and asks where he let her out. He says he took her to the Ferry Building, but on the way she wanted to hop out and grab a newspaper – a copy of the *Call*. Spade buys a copy himself but cannot see anything of relevance in it. He goes back to Brigid's room at the Coronet but cannot find anything. Returning to his office-building, Spade is met outside by the youth, who escorts him back to Gutman's suite at the Alexandria. After a brief struggle, Spade disarms the boy of two barely concealed pistols, pockets them, and knocks on Gutman's door.

CHAPTERS 13-16

Impressed by Spade's dexterity, Gutman begins to tell him the history of the bird: a bejewelled gold statuette presented by the Knights of Rhodes to Charles V (King of Spain and Holy Roman Emperor, 1500-1558), stolen by buccaneers, enamelled in black to hide its true value, and then passed from hand to hand through the centuries. Gutman found it in the possession of a Russian General in Constantinople and employed some agents to retrieve it – agents who then took it for themselves. Gutman believes that Brigid now has it, and Spade pretends that he knows where Brigid is, suggesting that he can get Gutman the bird in a few days' time. They both take a drink, and Spade soon realises that he has been drugged.

The next morning Spade returns to his office with a swollen head, unable to remember exactly what occurred after he passed out. He finds Effie waiting in his office, and asks her to contact her uncle, who is a history professor, and get him to check the accuracy of Gutman's narrative. In the lobby of Joel Cairo's hotel, Spade gets talking to the hotel detective, who lets him into Cairo's room. In the wastebasket he finds a copy of yesterday's edition of the *Call*, with a small bit torn out under the *"Arrived Today"* section (p. 132). He picks up a pristine copy from the *Call*'s business office, and reads that there is a ship called *La Paloma* arriving from Hong Kong at 8:05 that morning (p. 133). Back in his office, Spade telephones Tom Polhaus and arranges to have lunch with him, and then organizes a meeting with District Attorney Bryan. Effie's uncle has confirmed the dates of Gutman's story, and Effie also mentions that on her way back, she saw a boat on fire at the pier. Spade asks if she saw the boat's name, and she says yes: *"La Paloma"* (p. 135).

Spade and Tom Polhaus have lunch, and Polhaus reveals that the police now know for sure that Thursby shot Archer. Spade also discovers that Polhaus and Dundy only questioned Joel Cairo for a couple of hours – not all night, as Cairo had claimed. Spade goes on to his meeting with

District Attorney Bryan, who attempts to make Spade reveal the identity of his client, which Spade refuses.

Spade hunts for Gutman and Cairo, but has no luck. Finally Effie convinces him to go and investigate *La Paloma* in search of Brigid. Returning, he reports back what he has learned to Effie: that Brigid came aboard *La Paloma* yesterday afternoon to meet with its Captain, Jacobi. Later that evening, Cairo, Gutman and Gutman's boy (who we have learned is called Wilmer) turned up too. At some point in the evening a row was heard, and then a gunshot. Yet all five were seen to leave Jacobi's room in one piece, and have not been seen since. At this point, a tall man enters Spade's office carrying a "brown-wrapped parcel", before falling down dead (p. 153). The man, Captain Jacobi, has been shot multiple times. Spade opens the parcel and discovers the "foot-high figure of a bird, black as coal" (p. 154). Suddenly there is a telephone call from Brigid, who is at the Alexandria and seems to be in danger. Spade tells Effie to call the police and give them the full story, only leaving out the bird. Taking the statue with him, he heads for the Alexandria.

CHAPTERS 17-20

Spade checks the statue in at the parcel room of the Pickwick Stage terminal, and then carries on to the hotel. In Gutman's suite, he finds a girl – apparently Gutman's daughter – who seems to have been drugged. She tells him that Gutman, Cairo and Wilmer have taken Brigid to an address on Ancho Avenue. Spade calls an ambulance for the girl, and then heads over to the address, but once there he finds a completely empty house. He has been duped. Finally returning home, Brigid appears just outside his apartment and falls into his arms. They take the elevator up to his room, where they find Gutman, and Wilmer and Cairo both brandishing pistols.

Gutman offers Spade an envelope of money in exchange for the delivery of the bird, although it is less than was agreed upon: only 10 000 dollars. Spade reminds everyone that first they need a "fall-guy" to go down for Thursby and Jacobi's murders (p. 171). Spade suggests Wilmer, but Gutman claims that Wilmer is like a son to him. Then Spade suggests Cairo. Wilmer loses his temper and raises his gun, at which Gutman and

Cairo attempt to restrain him, and Spade knocks him out. Gutman finally agrees that Wilmer be the fall-guy.

Gutman fills in some details about what really happened. He and Cairo knew that Brigid somehow had the bird, and so Wilmer killed Thursby to scare her into cooperating – but this did not work. When Cairo read about the arrival of *La Paloma* from Hong Kong, he and Gutman realised that Brigid must have stowed the bird on board. The five of them all came to some agreement on *La Paloma*, but Brigid and Jacobi once again escaped them, and the next morning Wilmer caught Jacobi on his way out of Brigid's hotel and shot him. Jacobi nonetheless managed to escape with the bird, before arriving at Spade's office.

For all this time, Brigid has been holding on to the envelope with the 10 000 dollars in it, and taking it to give to Spade, Gutman notes that now it contains only 9000. Spade ushers Brigid into the bathroom and forces her to remove all her clothes to prove to him that she did not take the thousand dollar bill, which she reluctantly does. Spade's search turns up nothing. Gutman has played a joke on him, and removed one of the bills himself. At 7 o'clock Spade finally calls Effie and asks her to bring the bird over to them. Once it arrives, Gutman sticks a knife through the enamel and discovers underneath, not gold but lead – the bird is a fake. They realise that the Russian General must have made a duplicate bird. Gutman and Cairo decide to return to Constantinople to continue the search. Spade returns Gutman's 10 000 dollars, while taking one thousand-dollar bill for himself.

Spade and Brigid are left alone. Spade calls Tom Polhaus and tips him off about Wilmer, Gutman and Cairo, who are now returning to the Alexandria. Spade then reveals to Brigid that he knows it was she who killed Archer in an attempt to frame Thursby. Spade admits that he loves her, but nonetheless he must turn her in to the police. He later learns that Gutman has been shot dead by Wilmer.

CHARACTER STUDY

P.I. SAM SPADE

Hammett describes his private detective hero as looking "rather pleasantly like a blond satan" (p. 1). This description seems strange now, mainly because it so little resembles the physical qualities of Hollywood's quintessential noir private investigator, Humphrey Bogart. Bogart, who played Sam Spade in John Huston's 1941 film adaptation, was short, stocky and grizzled, with dark hair, and his countenance became synonymous in the popular imagination with that of the hard-drinking, tough-talking American detective of the 1940's. Sam Spade is one of the earliest and most influential manifestations of this mythic cultural figure. Even if he does not bear a physical resemblance to the Hollywood archetype, he exhibits all the same personality traits. He is honest, but he is no moral crusader either. He is not afraid to strike when struck, and he has little time or appetite for sentiment. He relies less on physical strength, though he certainly does not lack it, than on resourcefulness. He is a careful and canny forward-planner, as well as an improviser when the time demands.

BRIGID O'SHAUGHNESSY

Brigid is the prototypical *femme fatale*. She carefully manoeuvres throughout the novel, barely ever letting her carefully assumed mask of vulnerability slip. Underneath her dramatic pleas for assistance, she is clearly a canny operator, and the only character she cannot seem to run rings around is Spade. Like everyone trying to survive in a dog-eat-dog society, she uses whatever weapons she has in her arsenal, which for her are charm, sexuality, the power to evoke sympathy, and – when the time demands it – cool-headed violence.

JOEL CAIRO

Joel Cairo's character portrait might well prove troubling for a modern audience. His homosexuality is referenced repeatedly by other characters throughout the novel. When Spade searches his pockets he finds "three gaily colored silk handkerchiefs fragrant of *chypre*" (p. 45).

Hammett presents Cairo's sexuality as a kind of deviant and inferior form of masculinity, which overlaps with his racial otherness. Cairo is also Greek, and we can imagine that his skin is slightly darker than that of the other characters. These characteristics are meant to form a contrast with Spade, who is hyper-masculine, heterosexual and white.

CASPER GUTMAN

As his name implies, Casper Gutman is a large man. With him, Hammett paints a highly engaging and effective portrait of a man who has, in every way, too much of everything. He over-eats, he drinks a lot, he smokes cigars, and he clearly has a lot of money. He is also an aficionado of culture and history, and indeed of language: he loves the sound of his own voice, and is a connoisseur of fire-side conversation. He is an over-consumer, and like all over-consumers he will never be satisfied by his intake. Gutman's hunt for the Maltese Falcon is symbolic of an insatiable hunger that will ultimately consume him.

ANALYSIS

AMERICAN CRIME FICTION AND THE GREAT DEPRESSION

The Maltese Falcon was released in the early years of the Great Depression in America. In October 1929 the stock market at Wall Street had crashed, and during the 1930s unemployment in the United States rose to 25%. Hammett's novel is hardly a work of social realism – literature of the kind that authors such as John Steinbeck (American writer, 1902-1968) would write about the situation in 1930s America. But that does not mean that the socio-economic context of the time in which Hammett was writing is irrelevant. Considering *The Maltese Falcon*'s popularity, certain of its concerns and dynamics clearly spoke to its contemporary readership.

The world that Hammett presents is one in which everyone is driven by material concerns. Gutman, Cairo, Thursby and Brigid are after the bird not for antiquarian purposes; not for a love of history, or for the joy of adventure. Even Gutman, who is obviously a knowledgeable amateur historian and perhaps even considers himself an intellectual, has no interest in keeping the bird himself. He, like all the others, wants it for its economic value – so he can sell it on to the highest bidder, and live the rest of his life as a rich man. It is this materialistic motivation which drives all four characters. Even our protagonist Sam Spade is working for payment, and constantly adjusting his approach depending on how much money is on offer and from whom. One of the basic components of most drama is that different characters have different aims and motivations, which often lead to conflict. Detective stories frequently involve the unravelling of a hitherto obscured motive: some buried reason why x killed y. But what unites much of American crime fiction dating from around the time of the Great Depression is that there is only one motivation driving everyone: money.

This was the world that everyone saw in the America of the 1930's. It was a world that had apparently been bankrupted by the carelessness and greed of unrestrained capitalism, but that as it became poorer and poorer was obviously more and more desperate for money. In the absence of paid employment, crime can become a necessity when the choice lies between that and starvation.

Sam Spade emerges as the hero of *The Maltese Falcon* primarily through his relation to labour. Whatever we think of his methods, no-one can deny that he works hard for his money. It is difficult to tell, amongst all the action, when it is he actually manages to grab some sleep. He is tireless in his effort and attention, as well as in his physical movement around San Francisco. He seems to know the town like the back of his hand, and seems able to talk to anyone in it – he also knows exactly who to talk to. Spade perfectly understands how to manoeuvre through his own society, while also watching his back, and maintaining his own personal sense of integrity.

In an age of socio-economic stasis and powerlessness, the figure of the private investigator, and indeed of the *femme fatale*, emerge as potent cultural icons. They convey self-assurance, wit and street-smarts as well as rapid mobility – the ability to sail between class boundaries, while keeping themselves perfectly intact.

THE BIRTH OF FILM NOIR

The hard-boiled world that Dashiell Hammett created in novels like *The Maltese Falcon* would become a steadfast genre in 20th-century American culture. Fellow writers like Raymond Chandler, James M. Cain (American writer, 1892-1977) and Horace McCoy (American writer, 1897-1955) would follow in his footsteps, writing stories featuring tough-talking heroes that played out in the violent underworld of inner-city America. But Hammett's impact has been just as felt in the movies as it has been in the literary world.

The Maltese Falcon was adapted for film twice in the 1930s, and then again by director John Huston in 1941 in what has become an early and famous example of American film noir. Film noir was a term first used by Nino Frank (French film critic, 1904-1988) to describe a certain mode of dark Hollywood crime thriller produced in the 1940s. These films, made during the Second World War and often with constrained budgets, embraced the formal limitations of black and white photography and relied on darkness and chiaroscuro effects to create a sinister and moody atmosphere. This now iconic genre of Hollywood filmmaking is often thought of as a fusion of the world of American hard-boiled fiction with certain German Expressionist filming techniques.

A novel like *The Maltese Falcon*'s suitability for the screen is not entirely coincidental. Literary commentators at the time noted that contemporary American crime fiction in particular seemed pre-disposed to the cinematic eye – almost as though crime writers were designing their novels especially for Hollywood adaptation. Like a movie thriller, *The Maltese Falcon* is light on internal reflection and heavy on action and dialogue; events (and bodies) pile up like blows dealt in rapid succession, and we find ourselves reeling in an effort to keep up. Hammett's writing style is deft and sharp, and lends itself to being spoken aloud. He writes in the rhythms of everyday speech, in a language which is not over-literary or ostentatious – a democratic language, available to all.

On the one hand, it is natural that artists are influenced by developments in other mediums:

we should find it no surprise that Hammett's fiction has formal resonances with contemporary Hollywood filmmaking. On the other hand, this filmic influence on fiction certainly had an economic dimension as well. The Hollywood studios offered salaries that few writers could expect to earn through their fiction alone. A film adaptation of your novel, or even a job as a screenwriter, could represent a massive windfall for a writer. Indeed, some of the greatest American novelists of the 20th century ended up doing their stints in Hollywood writing films, including William Faulkner (American writer, 1897-1962) and F. Scott Fitzgerald (American writer, 1896-1940).

FURTHER REFLECTION

SOME QUESTIONS TO THINK ABOUT...

- How far might we read *The Maltese Falcon* as a Marxist novel?
- Hammett chooses a wacky array of names for his cast of characters: Sam Spade, Joel Cairo, Casper Gutman and Brigid O'Shaughnessy. What might be his reason for this? Are there any other names in the novel that might have playful double meanings?
- How does Hammett create excitement and suspense throughout his novel?
- Hammett gives titles to each of his 20 chapters. Why do you think he does this?
- What do you think is the pertinence of the story that Spade tells Brigid about the disappearance of Flitcraft? What is its effect within the novel's wider narrative?
- If we were to think of the Maltese Falcon as a symbol, what might it represent?

We want to hear from you!
Leave a comment on your online library
and share your favourite books on social media!

FURTHER READING

REFERENCE EDITION

- Hammett, D. (2010) *The Maltese Falcon.* London: Orion.

ADAPTATIONS

- *The Maltese Falcon.* (1931) [Film]. Roy Del Ruth. Dir. United States: Warner Bros.

- *Satan Met a Lady.* (1936) [Film]. William Dieterle. Dir. United States: Warner Bros.

- *The Maltese Falcon.* (1941) [Film]. John Huston. Dir. United States: Warner Bros.

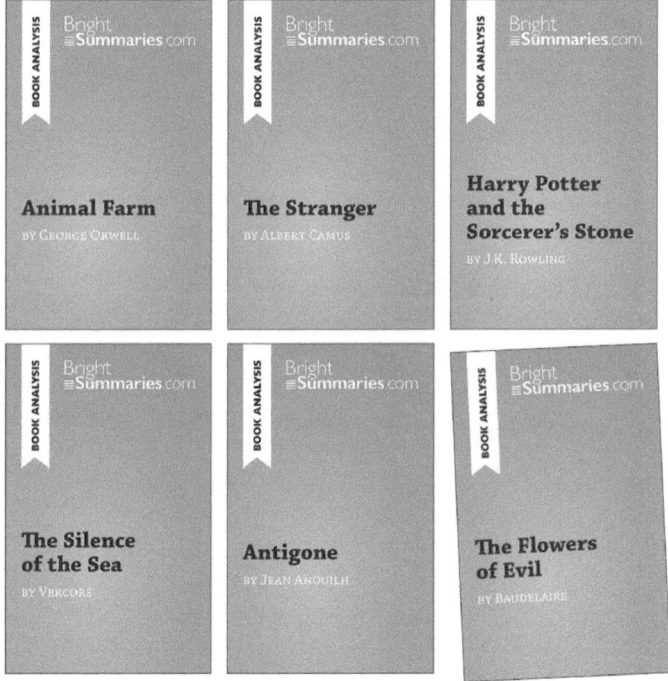

www.brightsummaries.com

Ebook EAN: 9782808018449

Paperback EAN: 9782808018456

Legal Deposit: D/2019/12603/89

Cover: © Primento

Digital conception by Primento, the digital partner of
publishers.